THE BIBLE IN YOUR HAND

MFON . EFFIONG TOCHUKWU

The Bible in Your Hand

An Inspirational Collection of Works in Praise of the Bible

Mfon . Effiong Tochukwu

Dreamstone Publishing 2015

www.dreamstonepublishing.com

ISBN: 1925165485

ISBN-13: 978-1-925165-48-7

DISCLAIMER

All works presented in this book have been collected by the author from varied sources. Where the original author of a work is known, they are attributed. All efforts have been made to confirm that material herein collected does not infringe any current copyright. Copyright on this work is asserted only on the design of this book, and the presentation of these materials collected in this specific collection and within this format, not on the origination of the works themselves.

DEDICATION

I dedicate this Book to the Almighty God, who made it possible and has given me the strength to forge ahead.

To my Lovely Wife Tochukwu Blessing Mfon, for her prayers and support

To my Adorable Children, Etido, Nyakdara, Utibe, Etiene. They are all wonderful children in making sure the environment is conducive and noise free.

HOLY BIBLE

INTRODUCTION

I am the owner of Insout Services, a life changing book reading and discussion group. The compilation of this book began when we were studying the book of the Old Testament, of which study I was the coordinator, and succeeding classes have seemed to enjoy and appreciated the collection.

Various classes stated that they would like to have these tributes in such form as would be readily available for reference - it was then that I decided to enlarge the collection and seek a publisher for the same.

When Kim Lambert of Dreamstone Publishing was consulted, she quickly agreed to publish this compilation, as she readily saw the possible help it could be to preachers, teachers, speakers, and many others perhaps.

This little volume is sent forth with a prayer that many shall read it and that it shall be the cause for them to have a greater love of, and a deeper appreciation for, God's Book - the Bible

M.E Tochukwu

POETRY

The poems in this section all focus on the Bible itself. They were written by very diverse people across centuries, yet have a common theme.

1. The Bible

We search the world for truth. We cull
The good, the true, the beautiful,
From graven stone and written scroll,
And all old flower-fields of the soul;
And, weary seekers of the best,
We come back laden from our quest,
To find that all the sages said
Is in the Book our mothers read.

John Greenleaf Whittier

2. The Book of Books

Within this ample volume lies
The mystery of mysteries.
To whom their God has given grace
To read, to fear, to hope, to pray,
To lift the latch, to force the way;
But better had they ne'er been born
Than read to doubt, or read to scorn.

Sir Walter Scott

3. The Precious Bible

Though the cover is worn
And the pages are torn,
And though places bear traces of tears,
Yet more precious than gold
Is the Book, worn and old,
That can shatter and scatter my fears.

When I prayerfully look
In the precious old Book,
Many pleasures and treasures I see;
Many tokens of love
From the Father above,
Who is nearest and dearest to me.

This old Book is my guide,
'Tis a friend by my side,
It will lighten and brighten my way;
And each promise I find
Soothes and gladdens my mind
As I read it and heed it today.

Anonymous

4. God's Word

I paused last eve beside the blacksmith's door,
And heard the anvil ring, the vesper's chime,
And looking in I saw upon the floor
Old hammers, worn with beating years of time.
"How many anvils have you had?" said I,
"To wear and batter all these hammers so?"
"Just one," he answered. Then with twinkling eye:
"The anvil wears the hammer out, you know."
And so, I thought, the anvil of God's Word
For ages skeptics' blows have beat upon,
But though the noise of falling blows was heard
The anvil is unchanged; the hammers gone.

John Clifford

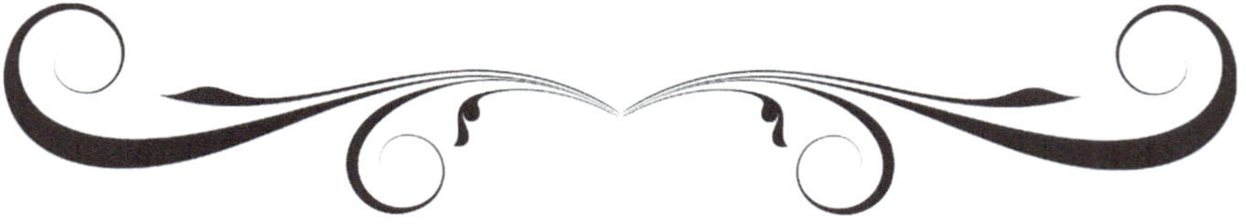

5. The Quest Eternal

For man's unceasing quest for God,
For God's unceasing quest for man,
For records of his love and power
Surrounding life since life began
We thank thee, Lord most high.
For ancient tales of long ago,
Man's guesses when the world was young;
For talks around the blazing fire,
For stories told and stories sung,
We thank thee, Lord most high.
For those great laws the Hebrews made,
Among the greatest ever known,
For early history wise men wrote,
Engraved on parchment, skin, or stone.
We thank thee, Lord most high.
For those old songs of tuneful verse,
The music of the shepherd king,
For songs the Boy of Nazareth sang,
And still succeeding ages sing,
We thank thee, Lord most high.

Alice M. Pullen

6. O' Word of God Incarnate

O' Word of God incarnate,
O' Wisdom from on high,
O' Truth unchanged, unchanging,
O' Light of our dark sky,
We praise Thee for the radiance
That from the hallowed page,
A lantern of our footsteps,
Shines on from age to age.

The Church from her dear Master
Received the gift divine,
And still that light she lifteth
O'er all the earth to shine.
It is the golden casket,
Where gems of truth are stored;
It is the heaven-drawn picture
Of Christ, the living Word.

It floateth like a banner
Before God's host unfurled;
It shineth like a beacon
Above the darkling world;
It is the chart and compass

That o'er life's surging sea,
'Mid mists and rocks and quick-sands,
Still guides, 0 Christ, to Thee.

O make Thy Church, dear Saviour,
A lamp of purest gold,
To bear before the nations
Thy true light, as of old.
O teach Thy wandering pilgrims
By this their path to trace,
Till, clouds and darkness ended,
They see Thee face to face.

William Waisham How

7. My Bible

I love the dear old Bible
The Word of Christian life,
For it's my shield and buckler,
And sword in mortal strife.

It tells me of my Saviour,
And shows the path to go;
It tells me of God's heaven
And much I want to know

It is my boon companion,
A keeper by my side;
It is my daily comfort
And never failing guide.

I'll cherish it and love it
Until I see the Lord,
And tell men of its message
God's will within His Word.

Anonymous

8. Lamp of Our Feet

Lamp of our feet, whereby we trace
Our path when we want to stray;
Stream from the fount of heavenly grace
Brook by the traveler's way.

Word of the everlasting God,
Will of his glorious Son;
Without thee how could earth be trod
Or heaven itself be won?

Lord, grant us all a right to learn
The wisdom it imparts;
And to its heavenly teaching turn
With simple, child-like hearts.

Bernard Barton

9. A Bit of the Book

A bit of the Book in the morning,
To order my onward way.
A bit of the Book in the evening,
To hallow the end of the day.

Margaret E. Sangster

10. The Bible

It is an armory of light;
Let constant use but keep it bright
You'll find it yields
To holy hands and humble hearts,
More swords and shields
Than sin hath snares, or
Hell hath darts.

Richard Crashaw

11. The Word

The Word unto the prophet spoken
Was writ on tablets yet unbroken:
The Word by seers or sibyls told,
In groves of oak, or fanes of gold,
Still floats upon the morning wind,
Still whispers to the willing mind.

Ralph Waldo Emerson

12. My Bible

And should my soul be torn with grief
Upon my shelf I find
A little volume torn and thumbed,
For comfort just designed.
I take my little Bible down

And read its pages o'er,
And when I part from it I find
I'm stronger than before.

Edgar A. Guest

13. The Book of Books

The Bible is the Book of books,
As far above all other books
As Heaven is higher than the earth
For Heaven alone could give it birth.

Tis purer than the purest gold
It is a mine of wealth untold:
God's gracious Love it doth display
Toward all who seek, believe, obey.

This Book of books, God's Living Word,
Thus thrills with the story of our Lord.
In all mankind new hope doth spring
Through Jesus, Saviour, coming king!
So beautiful, wonderful, true; Book of Ages--
Old - yet new.

Anonymous

14. It's All in the Bible

From page to page from the front
to the back of the cover,
The black letters, the red ones, all these
teach God is the true lover;

The black, the yellow the red and
also the white,
God watches over us all when we
sleep at night,
'Cause we're His children whether in
comfort or in need
It's all in the Bible, if you'll take
the time to read.

Anonymous

15. My Bible and I

(John 3:31 and Psalm 119)

We've traveled together,
My Bible and I,
Through all kinds of weather,
With smile or with sigh!
In sorrow or sunshine,
In tempest or calm!
Thy friendship changing,
My lamp and my psalm.

We've traveled together,
My Bible and I,
When life had grown weary,
And death e'en was nigh!
But all through the darkness
Of mist or of wrong,
I found there a solace,
A prayer and a song,

So now who shall part us,
My Bible and I?
Shall “isms” or schisms,
Or “new lights” who try?
Shall shadow for substance
Or stone for good bread.

Supplant thy Sound wisdom,
Give folly instead?

Ah, no, my dear Bible,
Exponent of light!
Thou sword of the spirit,
Put error to flight!
And still through life’s journey,
Until my last sign,
We’ll travel together,
My Bible and I.

Charles Sandford

16. Thy word is a lamp to my feet

Thy Word is a lamp to my feet,
A light to my path alway,
To guide and to save me from sin,
And show me the heavenly way.

Refrain

Thy Word have I hid in my heart,
That I might not sin against Thee,
That I might not sin, That I might not sin,
Thy Word have I hid in my heart.

Forever O Lord, is Thy Word
Established and fix'd on high;
Thy faithfulness unto all men
Abideth forever nigh.

Refrain

At morning, at noon, and at night,

I ever will give Thee praise;

For Thou art my portion, O Lord

And shalt he thro' il1 my days.

Refrain

Ernest O. Sellers

17. The Book

Softly I closed the Book as in a dream
And let its echoes linger to redeem
Silence with music, darkness with its gleam.

That day I worked no more. I could not bring
My hands to toil, my thoughts to trafficking.
A new light shone on every common thing.

Celestial glories flamed before my gaze.
That day I worked no more. But, to God's praise,
I shall work better au my other days.

Winfred Ernest Garrison

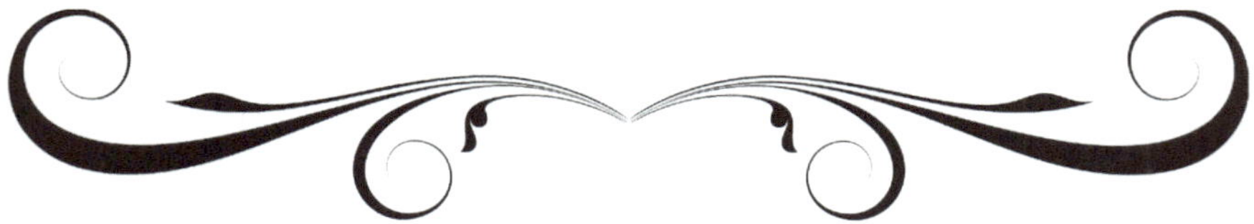

18. Holy Bible, Book Divine

Holy Bible, Book divine,
Precious treasure, thou art mine:
Mine to tell me whence I came;
Mine to teach me what I am.

Mine to chide me when I rove,
Mine to show a Saviour's love;
Mine thou art to guide and guard;
Mine to punish or reward.

Mine to comfort in distress,
Suffering in this wilderness;
Mine to show, by living faith,
Man can triumph over death.

Mine to tell of joys to come,
And the rebel sinner's doom:
O thou holy Book divine,
Precious treasure, thou art mine.

John Burton, Sr.

SONGS

The songs in this section celebrate the Bible and its words.

19. How Firm a Foundation

How firm a foundation, ye saints of the Lord,
Is laid for your faith in His excellent Word!
What more can He say than to you He hath said,
You who unto Jesus for refuge have fled?

In every condition, in sickness, in health,
In poverty's vale or abounding in wealth;
At home and abroad, on the land, on the sea;
As your days may demand, shall your strength ever be.

When through fiery trials thy pathway shall lie,
My grace, all sufficient, shall be thy supply;

The flame shall not hurt thee;
I only design Thy dross to consume, and thy gold to refine.

E'en down to old age, all My people shall prove
My sovereign, eternal, unchangeable love;
And when hoary hairs shall their temples adorn,
Like lambs they shall still in My bosom be borne.

The soul that on Jesus hath leaned for repose,
I will not, I will not desert to its foes;
That soul, though all hell should endeavor to shake,
I'll never, no, never, no, never forsake!

George Keith

20. Wonderful Words of Life

Sing them over again to me,
Wonderful words of Life;
Let me more of their beauty see,
Wonderful words of Life.
Words of life and beauty,
Teach me faith and duty:
Beautiful words, wonderful words,
Wonderful words of Life.

Christ, the blessed One, gives to all,
Wonderful words of Life
Sinner, list to the loving call,
Wonderful words of Life.
All so freely given,
Wooing us to heaven:
Beautiful words, wonderful words,
Wonderful words of Life.

Sweetly echo the gospel call,

Wonderful words of Life;

Offer pardon and peace to all,

Wonderful words of Life.

Jesus, only Saviour,

Sanctify forever:

Beautiful words, wonderful words,

Wonderful words of Life.

Phillip. P. Bliss

21. Standing on the Promise

Standing on the promises of Christ my King,
Thro' eternal ages let His praises ring;
Glory in the highest, I will shout and sing,
Standing on the promises of God.

Chorus

Standing, standing,
Standing on the promises of God my Saviour;
Standing, standing,
I'm standing on the promises of God.

Standing on the promises that cannot fail,
When the howling storms of doubt and fear assail,
By the living word of God I shall prevail,
Standing on the promises of God.

Chorus

Standing on the promises of Christ the Lord,
Bound to Him eternally by love's strong cord,
Overcoming daily with the Spirit's sword,
Standing on the promises of God.
Standing on the promises I cannot fall,
Listening every moment to the Spirit's call,
Resting in my Saviour, as my all in all,
Standing on the promises of God.

Chorus

R. Kelso Carter

22. Break Thou the Bread of Life

Break Thou the bread of life,
Dear Lord, to me,
As Thou didst break the loaves
Beside the sea;
Beyond the sacred page
I seek Thee Lord;
My spirit pants for Thee,
O living Word.

Bless Thou the truth, dear Lord,
To me, to me,
As Thou didst bless the bread
By Galilee;
Then shall all bondage cease,
All fetters fall;
And I shall find my peace,
My All in all.

Thou art the bread of life
O Lord, to me,
Thy holy Word the Truth
That saveth me;
Give me to eat and live
With Thee above;
Teach me to love Thy truth,
For Thou art love.

O send Thy Spirit Lord,
Now unto me,
That He may touch my eyes,
And make me see;
Show me the truth concealed
Within Thy Word,
And in Thy Book revealed
I see the Lord.

Mary Ann Lathbury.

23. I Know the Bible Is True

I know the Bible was sent from God,
The Old, as well as the New;
Inspired and holy, the living Word,
I know the Bible is true.

Refrain
I know, I know,
I know the Bible is ture;
Divinely inspired the whole way thro',
I know the Bible is true.

I know the story of Christ is true,
His virgin, glorious birth,
His life, His death, and the open tomb,
And His return to the earth.

Refrain

I know the Bible is wholly true,
For peace it gave me within;
It finds me, comforts me day by day,
And gives me vict'ry o'er sin.

Refrain

Tho' foes deny with a spirit bold
The message old, but still new,
Its truth is sweeter each time 'tis told,
I know the Bible is true.

Refrain

Bavlus- Benjamin McKinney

24. My Mother's Bible

There's a dear and precious Book,
Tho' it's worn and faded now,
Which recalls those happy days of long ago;
When I stood at mother's knee,
With her hand upon my brow,
And I heard her voice in gentle tones and low.

Refrain
Blessed Book, precious Book,
On thy dear old tear-stained leaves I love to look;
Thou art sweeter day by day,
As I walk the narrow way
That leads at last to that bright home above.

As she read the stories o'er,
Of those mighty men of old,
Of Joseph and of Daniel and their trials;
Of David bold,
Who became a king at last;
Of Satan with his many wicked wiles.

Refrain

Then she read of Jesus' love,
As He blest the children dear,
How He suffered, bled and died upon the tree;
Of His heavy load of care,
Then she dried my flowing tears
With her kisses as she said it was for me.

Refrain

Well, those days are past and gone,
But their mem'ry lingers still,
And the dear old Book each day has been my guide;
And I seek to do His will,
As my mother taught me then,
And ever in my heart His words abide.

Milan Bertrand Williams

25. Thy Word Is Like a Garden, Lord

Thy Word is like a garden, Lord,
With flowers bright and fair;
And ev'ry one who seeks may pluck
A lovely cluster there.
Thy Word is like a deep, deep mine;
And jewels rich and rare
Are hidden in its mighty depths
For ev'ry searcher there.

Thy Word is like a starry host;
A thousand rays of light
Are seen to guide the traveler
And make his pathway bright.

O may I live Thy precious Word,
May I explore the mine,
May I the fragrant flowers glean,
May light upon me shine.

Edwin Hodder

HOLY
BIBLE

HOLY
BIBLE

PROSE

This section contains quotes and short prose pieces, all focused on the Bible, its words and its values.

26. The Tree of Knowledge

The Bible contains 3,566,480 letters, 810,697 words, 31,175 verses, 1189 chapters, and 66 books.

The longest chapter is the 119th Psalm; the shortest and middle chapter is the 117th Psalm.

The middle verse is the 8th of the 118th Psalm.

The longest name is in the 8th of the 118th Psalm.

The longest name is in the 8th chapter of Isaiah.

The word "and" occurs 46,627 times, the word "Lord" 1855 times.

The 37th chapter of Isaiah and the 19th chapter of the 2nd book of Kings are alike.

The longest verse is the 9th of the 8th chapter of Esther; the shortest verse is the 35th of the 11th chapter of John.

In the 21st verse of the 7th chapter of Ezra is the alphabet.

The finest piece of reading is the 26th chapter of Acts.

The name of God is not mentioned in the book of Esther.

It contains knowledge, wisdom, holiness and love

Anonymous

27. I Am the Bible

I am the Bible. I am a library of sixty-six books. I am the world's best seller.

I am more than a mere book. I am a force that overpowers opposing systems of thought.

I am the rock upon which civil liberties and social freedom rest.

I answer the question: Who and where is God?

I was written by minds saturated with consciousness of God.

I am published in more languages and dialects than any other book that has ever been written.

I am cherished by millions of people as being the only concretely available and infallible rule of faith and practice.

I am the Word of God as set forth by inspired prophet, lawgiver, genealogist, priest, historian, poet, essayist, story-writer, moralist, seer, and theologian.

I set forth the way of life that leads to abundance and satisfaction of experience.

I tell the story of the great drama of redemption.

I am the meeting point of man's effort to discover God and God's revelation of Himself to man.

I inspire devotion to truth and purity of life purpose.

Norman E. Richardson

28. Packing

A young Christian packing his bag for a journey said to a friend, "I have nearly finished packing. All I have to put in are....

a guidebook,

a lamp,

a mirror,

a microscope,

a telescope,

a volume of fine poetry,

a few biographies,

a package of old letters,

a book of songs,

a sword,

a hammer, and

a set of tools."

"But you cannot put all that into your bag," objected the friend. "Oh, yes," said the Christian. "Here it is." And he placed his Bible in the corner of the suitcase and closed the lid.

Anonymous

29. The Mind of God

This book contains: The mind of God, the state of man, the way of salvation, the doom of sinners, and the happiness of believers.

Its doctrine is holy, its precepts are binding, its histories are true, and its decisions are immutable.

Read it to be wise, believe it to be safe, and practice it to be holy.

It contains light to direct you, food to support you and comfort to cheer you.

It is the traveler's map, the pilgrim's staff, the pilot's compass, the soldier's sword, and the Christian's charger.

Here heaven is opened, and the gates of hell disclosed.

Christ is its grand subject, and our good its design, and the glory of God its end.

It should fill the memory, rule the heart, and guide the feet. Read it slowly, frequently, and prayerfully.

It is a mine of wealth, health to the soul, and a river of pleasure.

It is given to you here in this life, will be opened at the judgment, and is established forever.

It involves the highest responsibility, will reward the greatest labor, and will condemn all who trifle with its sacred contents.

Anonymous

30.

To what greater inspiration and counsel can we turn than to the imperishable truth to be found in this treasure house, the Bible?

Queen Elizabeth II

31.

Unless we form the habit of going to the Bible in bright moments as well as in trouble, we cannot fully respond to its consolations because we lack equilibrium between light and darkness.

Helen Keller

32.

The Bible is the Book of life. Its aim is to interpret the living God to men.

Clifton J. Allen

33.

The Bible: This book will keep you from sin, or sin will keep you from this book.

Anonymous

34.

All human discoveries seem to be made only for the purpose of confirming more and more strongly the truths contained in the sacred scriptures.

Sir William Herschel

35.

Almost every man who has by his life work added to the sum of human achievements of which the race is proud has based his life work largely upon the teachings of the Bible.

Theodore Roosevelt

36.

It is impossible to rightly govern the world without God and the Bible.

George Washington

37.

The Bible: The window in this prison of hope through which we look into eternity.

John Sullivan Dwight

38.

The English Bible: A book which, if everything else in our language should perish, would alone suffice to show the whole extent of its beauty and power.

Thomas B. Macaulay

39.

The Bible is no mere book, but a living creature with a power that conquers all that oppose it.

Napoleon Bonaparte

40.

I believe the Bible is the best gift God has ever given to man. All the good from the Savior of the world is communicated to us through this book.

Abraham Lincoln

41.

This book is the secret of England's greatness.

Queen Victoria

42.

I have always said and always will say, that the studious perusal of the Bible will make better citizens, better husbands, and better fathers.

Thomas Jefferson

43.

My daily advisor and comfort is the impregnable Rock of the Holy Scriptures.

William Gladstone

44.

I am profitably engaged in reading the Bible. Take all of this book upon reason that you can, and the balance on faith, and you will live and die a better man.

Abraham Lincoln

45.

The Bible is the rock on which our republic rests.

Andrew Jackson

46.

There is not a community which cannot be purified, redeemed and improved by a broader knowledge and larger application of the Bible.

W. J. Bryan

47.

I am sorry for the men who do not read the Bible daily. I wonder why they deprive themselves of the strength and the pleasure.

I should be afraid to go forward if I did not believe that there lay at the foundation of all our schooling and all of our thought this incomparable and unimpeachable Word of God.

Woodrow Wilson

48.

Who kills a man, kills a reasonable creature, God's image; But he who destroys the good book, kills reason itself.

John Milton

49.

I thoroughly believe in a university education for both men and women; but I believe a knowledge of the Bible without a college course is more valuable than a college course without the Bible.

William Lyon Phelps

50.

It is a Book of books: The Bible out-shines all other books in the literary firmament, as the sun out-splendors the planets that move in their orbits around him.

It is a book full of history, geography, archaeology, prophecy, doctrine, exceeding, great and precious promises.

Anonymous

51.

I owe much to many, but I owe most to God, for I know that He is my best friend and my Bible is the greatest book I'll ever own.

Vonda Kay Van Dyke
Miss America of 1965

52.

Every soldier and sailor of these United States should have a Testament... we plead for a closer, wider and deeper study of the Bible, so that our people may be in fact, as well as in theory, doers of the Word and not hearers only."

Theodore Roosevelt

53.

The Bible is the book of all others to be read at all ages and in all conditions of human life. I speak as a man of the world, and I say to you, "Search the Scriptures."

John Quincy Adams

54.

It is a plain old book modest as nature itself, and as simple, too; a book of an unpretending work-day appearance, like the sun that warms, or the bread that nourishes us. And the name of this book is simply, 'The Bible'.

Heinrich Heine

55.

I have known ninety-five of the world's great men in my time, and of these eighty-seven were followers of the Bible. The Bible is stamped with a Specialty of Origin, and an immeasurable distance separates it from all competitors.

William Gladstone

56.

I believe every word in the Bible. I accept everything between the lids of the Book. I have good reason for my faith.

Sam P. Jones

57.

The Bible is a book of faith, and a book of doctrine, and a book of morals, and a book of religion, of special revelation from God; but it is also a book which teaches man his own dignity, and his equality with his fellowman.

Daniel Webster

58.

The Bible is the truest utterance that ever came by alphabetic, letters from the soul of man, through a window divinely opened, all men can look into the stillness of eternity, and discern in glimpses their far distant, long forgotten home.

Thomas Carlyle

59.

The grand old Book still stands; and this old earth, the more its leaves are turned and pondered, the more it will sustain and illustrate the pages of the Sacred Word.

Charles A. Dana

60.

The Bible is worth all other books which have ever been printed

Patrick Henry

61.

The Bible is the sheet-anchor of our liberties.

Ulysses. S. Grant

62.

Whatever merit there is in anything that I have written is simply due to the fact that when I was a child my mother daily read me a part of the Bible and daily made me learn a part of it by heart.

John Ruskin

63.

The Bible has been the Magna Charta of the poor and oppressed. The human race is not in a position to dispense with it.

Thomas Huxley

64.

The whole hope of human progress is suspended on the ever growing influence of the Bible.

William Henry Seward

65.

Bible reading is an education in itself.

Lord Tennyson

66.

It is impossible to enslave mentally or socially a Bible-reading people.

The principles of the Bible are the groundwork of human freedom.

Horace Greeley

67.

In all my perplexities and distresses, the Bible has never failed to give me light and strength.

Robert E. Lee

68.

There are more sure marks of authenticity in the Bible than in any profane history.

Sir Isaac Newton

69.

Let mental culture go on advancing, let the natural sciences progress in ever greater extent and depth, and the human mind widen itself as much as it desires; beyond the elevation and moral culture of Christianity, as it shines forth in the gospels, it will not go.

Johann Wolfgang von Goethe

70.

The existence of the Bible, as a book for the people, is the greatest benefit which the human race has ever experienced. Every attempt to belittle it is a crime against humanity.

Immanuel Kant

71.

The New Testament is the very best book that ever was or ever will be known in the world.

Charles Dickens

72.

The history of every individual man should be a Bible.

Navalis

73.

To me the greatest thing that has happened on this earth of ours is the rise of the human race to the vision of God.

That story of the human rise to what I call the vision of God is the story which is told in the Bible.

Jan Christian Smuts

74.

The Bible has made an ineffaceable impression upon child life.

Upon it poets have fed their genius.

Its thoughts lie like threads of gold upon the rich pages of each Macaulay or Burke.

Orators have quoted from it so largely that we may say that, in proportion as men are cultured, have they been students of the Bible.

Today its moral principles form the very substance and body of modern law and jurisprudence.

For centuries it has been the book for patriots and reformers; it has been the slave's book; it has been the book for the common people struggling upward: it has been the book of hope for all prodigals; it has been a medicine book for the heart broken, while its ideas furnish goals for society's future progress.

For the individual it teaches the art of individual worth, and is a guide to conduct and character.

For the state it is a handbook of universal civilization.

Newell Dwight Hillis

75.

So great is my veneration for the Bible that the earlier my children begin to read it the more confident will be my hope that they will prove useful citizens of their country and respectable members of society. I have for many years made it a practice to read through the Bible once every year.

John Quincy Adams

76.

The Bible resembles an extensive and highly cultivated flower garden, where there is a vast variety and profusion of fruits and flowers, some of which are more essential or more splendid than others; but there is not a blade suffered to grow in it which has not its use and beauty in the system.

Salvation for sinners is the grand truth presented everywhere, and in all points of light; but the pure in heart sees a thousand traits of the Divine character, of himself, and of the world: some striking and bold others cast as it were into the shade, and designed to be searched for and examined; some direct, others by way of intimation or inference.

Richard Cecil

77.

In this one book are the two most interesting personalities in the whole world God and yourself. The Bible is the story of God and man, a love story in which you and I must write our own ending, our unfinished autobiography of the creature and the Creator.

Fulton Oursier

78.

The Bible as a book stands alone. There never was, nor ever will be, another like it. As there is but one sun to enlighten the world spiritually. May that Book become to each of us the man of our counsel, the guide of our journey, the inspiration of our thought, and our support and comfort in life and in death.

A. Galloway

79.

The study of God's word, for the purpose of discovering God's will, is the secret discipline which has formed the greatest characters.

James Waddel Alexander

80. Truth without Mixture

The Scriptures of the Old and New Testaments were given by inspiration of God. Their content is, therefore, truth without any mixture of error; and they constitute the only sufficient, certain, and authoritative source of saving knowledge and rule of obedience and faith.

A statement of Fundamental Christian Principles

81.

We may compare the Bible to the Old Testament Tabernacle in the wilderness with its three courts. The outer court is the letter of the Scripture, the inner court, or holy place, is the truth of the Scripture; the holiest place of all is the person of Jesus Christ; and only when we pass the inmost veil do we come to Him.

A. T. Pierson

82.

The foundations of our society and our government rest so much on the teachings of the Bible that it would be difficult to support them if faith in these teachings should cease to be practically universal in our country.

Calvin Coolidge

83.

No other book has been thought about, written about, has so inspired other works to unfold its principles, as has the Bible.

When we compare the number of books dealing with all other religions with treatises on the Bible, we come to realize the place of the Bible in the thought of the world.

Have men written about Socrates, Plato, Aristotle, Caesar, Aurelius, Charlemagne, Alexander and Napoleon as they have written about Jesus Christ?

No other book has so gripped the thought and affections of man; no other book has so compelled attention to its truths; no other book has caused such personal concern regarding the great issues of life and death; no other book has so stirred the soul to its depths.

James H. Kay, Ph. D. LL.D.

84.

England has two books, one which she has made and one which has made her: Shakespeare and the Bible.

Victor Hugo

85.

I know the Bible is inspired because it inspires me.

Dwight L. Moody

86.

What other men learned from books, he with the aid only of his Bible, spelt out and put together by the light from heaven that irradiated his darkness.

He thought in the very dialect of Scripture; and the imagery of the Bible was every present to his thoughts, as, if we may say so, the native scenery of his spiritual birth.

He was made by the Bible; educated by the study of it; it was his "book of all learning;" and the simplicity of purpose and the intense interest with which he searched its contents, as the treasury of heavenly wisdom, rendered him, like Apollos, "eloquent and mighty in the Scriptures," while his mind became more and more imbued with their "spirit and life."

"Memoir of the Life and

Writings of John Bunyan"

87.

A stream where alike the elephant may swim and the lamb may wade.

Pope Gregory I

88.

The Scriptures teach us the best way of living, the noblest way of suffering, and the most comfortable way of dying.

John Flavel

89. Universal and Timeless

Born in the East and clothed in Oriental form and imagery, the Bible walks the ways of all the world with familiar feet and enters land after land to find its own everywhere.

It has learned to speak in hundreds of languages to the heart of man.

It comes into the palace to tell the monarch that he is a servant of the Most High, and into the cottage to assure the peasant that he is a son of God.

Children listen to its stories with wonder and delight, and wise men ponder them as parables of life. It has a word for peace for the time of peril, a word of comfort for the time of calamity, a word of light for the hour of darkness.

Its oracles are repeated in the assembly of the people, and its counsels whispered in the ear of the lonely.

The wicked and the proud tremble at its warnings, but to the wounded and the penitent it has a mother's voice.

The wilderness and the solitary place have been made glad by it, and the fire on the hearth has lit the reading of its well-worn pages.

It has woven itself into our dearest dreams, so that love, friendship, sympathy and devotion, memory and hope, put on the beautiful garments of its treasured speech, breathing of frankincense and myrrh.

No man is poor or desolate who has this treasure for his own.

When the landscape darkens and the trembling pilgrim comes to the valley named shadow, he is not afraid to enter; he takes the rod and staff of Scripture in his hand and says to his friend and comrade, “Goodbye, we shall meet again.” Comforted by that support, he goes toward the lonely pass as one who walks through darkness into light.

Henry Van Dyke

90. The Bible Works

The Bible works. Its truths transform the hearts and lives of men and women. It converts to a better life the small and the great.

The beggar on the street and the king on his throne, the poor woman weeping in an attic room and the philosopher in his endowed chair, the profoundest thinker and the uncultured savage are all changed by the power of this Book.

The drunkard, the thief, the libertine leave their sin to walk in the light of God's precepts.

The proud atheist becomes a humble believer in Christ by the truths of the Bible.

Dr. W. A. Criswell

91.

The Bible is the book above and beyond all books; as a river is beyond a nil in reach, as the sun is beyond a tallow candle in brightness, as an orchard is beyond a twig in fruit bearing, as Niagara is beyond a mud puddle in glory.

The Bible is the staff upon which millions of pilgrims have gone the weapons with which Christian soldiers have fought their battles to glorious victory, the compass that has guided men in darkness and distress.

Dr. R. G. Lee

92. Unity

The Bible is a unit. The Bible was written by approximately fifty-seven different authors from all walks of life farmers, shepherds, tentmakers, physicians, governors, and kings.

The span of its writing was about fifteen hundred years in places ranging all the way from Babylon to Rome. It deals with history, law, poetry, prophecy, philosophy, science, sociology, and salvation, to mention only a few of its varied themes.

The Bible was not written by its authors with the purpose of forming one book. Yet, gathered together under the guidance of the Holy Spirit in its final form after A. D. 300, it tells one complete story.

If one should read the New Testament without a knowledge of the Old Testament, he would ask, “Where is that which went before?”

If he should read the Old Testament without knowing the New Testament, he would inquire, “Where is the rest of the story?” The only reasonable answer is that all this was done under the guiding hand of God.

Herschel H. Hobbs

93. A Trip Through The Bible

With the Holy Spirit as my guide I entered the Wonderful temple of Christianity. I entered at the portico of Genesis, walked down through the Old Testament art galleries where the pictures of Noah, Abraham, Moses, Joseph, Isaac, Jacob, and Daniel hung on the wall.

I walked into the music room of Psalms, where the Spirit swept the keyboard of nature until it seemed that every reed and pipe in God's great organ responded to the tuneful harp of David, the sweet singer of Israel.

I entered the chamber of Ecclesiastes, where the voice of the preacher was heard and into the conservatory of Sharon and the Lily-of-the-Valley's sweet scented spices filled and perfumed my life.

I entered the business of Proverbs and then into the observatory room of the prophets, where I saw telescopes of various sizes pointed to far-off events but all concentrated upon the bright and morning star which was to rise over the hills of Judea for our Salvation.

I entered the audience room of the King of Kings and caught a vision of His glory from the standpoint of Matthew, Mark, Luke, and John; walked in the Acts of the Apostles, where the Holy Spirit was doing His work in the formation of the infant Church.

Then, into the correspondence room where Paul, Peter, James and John prepared their Epistles.I stepped into the throne room of Revelation, where towered the glittering throne, and caught a vision of the king sitting at the right hand of God, in all His Glory, and I cried,

"All hail the power of Jesus' name.

Let angels prostrate fall

Bring forth the royal diadem And Crown Him Lord of All!"

Billy Sunday

94. A Perfect Treasure

We believe that the Holy Bible was written by men inspired, and is a perfect treasure of heavenly instruction:

that it has God for its author, salvation for its end, and truth without any mixture of error for its matter; that it reveals the principles by which God will judge us; and therefore is, and shall remain to the end of the world, the true center of Christian union, and the supreme standard by which all human conduct, creeds, and opinions should be tried.

J. Newton Brown

95. The Bible - a Divine Book

1. Its acceptance by Christians Strong proof.

(1) Christians from the Apostolic Fathers of today have always believed it to be God's revelation.

(2) They are the best witnesses they have the best chance to test its divine import.

(3) Unreasonable to reject the testimony of the best men of all ages for that of less competent witnesses.

2. Its formation and unity.

(1) Product of various ages of the world, written over a period of seventeen centuries.

(2) Product of more than forty men among whom were shepherds, fishermen, priests, warriors, kings, and statesmen some from the city, some were from the country, some educated, some uneducated, living in distant ages, one not knowing of the writing of the other But wrote 66 books that agree and grew into a perfect whole.

3. Its preservation.

(1) Preserved by the Jews whom it constantly condemns.

(2) Preserved while other great books and libraries perished, most of them living but a little while.

(3) Preserved although individual and organized infidelity and certain organized governments tried to destroy it only a divine book could survive.

4. Its solution of man's difficulties Answers the questions.

(1) What is the origin of the world?

(2) What is the origin of man? What is he and where is he going?

(3) What is the origin of sin?

(4) Will sin be punished to satisfy life's unfairness?

(5) Is there redemption how and by whom?

(6) Is there a future state?

(7) All we know concerning these things is pure guess work except the Bible answers they satisfy.

5. Its fairness and candor.

(1) Does not exaggerate.

(2) Tells faults as well as virtues of its heroes. It judges the soul contradicting its passions, revealing its guilt, and humbling its pride.

(3) Man would not write such a book if he could, and could not if he would.

6. Its richness and universality of teaching.

(1) Furnishes the highest standards of living for men and nations in every age.

(2) Each new generation finds new and wonderful treasures.

(3) Has inspired thousands of books

7. Its historical accuracy.

(1) In thousands of references to towns, cities, battles, kings, empires, generals and great events no mistakes are found.

(2) Corroborative evidence has been found as to its stories of creation and fall of man, the flood, tower of Babel, bondage in Egypt, captivity, and many other things.

(3) It has none of the historical bias of human histories. All this marks it as a divine book.

8. Its spiritual character.

(1) The spirit of the Bible is too high above man for him to have originated it.

(2) It satisfies the spiritual longing of man while mere human writings do not satisfy.

9. Its scientific accuracy.

(1) The Bible does not claim to be a book of science; yet science has not shown any fairly interpreted passage of scripture to be untrue.

(2) It contains none of the crude superstitions existing when it was written, such as the earth resting on a table or carried on the shoulders of a giant.

(3) It is true to science when it touches it

a. As to many special matters -- the earth has a circuit**, Isa. 40:22;** the earth has an invisible support, **Job 26:7**; the sun travels in a circuit, **Psa. 19:6;** the wind has weight, **Job 28:25;** the whole matter of rain and evaporation, **Eccl. 1:7, Job 36:26-28;** the currents of the wind, **Eecl. 1:6.**

b. As to the order of creation -- Most simple and less important first.

c. There are no contradictions --The God of the Bible and nature seems to be the same.

10. Its prophetic accuracy.

(1) Hundreds of predictions touching persons and nations such as Israel, Egypt, Babylon, Edon, Syria, and Judah and many cities large and small made by twenty or more men all came true.

(2) Jesus made many such predictions, as to His death and resurrection and destruction of Jerusalem. They too came true. A book that foretells the future is more than a human book.

11. Its miracles.

(1) The miracles of the Bible are far superior to the so called miracles of mythology.

(2) Never performed for the benefit of the one doing it as is the case of false or counterfeit miracles.

(3) They are performed for the good of others -- Healing the sick, lame, blind, deaf, etc. all for the glory of God.

12. Its fruit - a worthy test.

(1) It touches and cleanses our lives and carries enlightenment and civilization with it everywhere.

(2) It reclaims confirmed drunkards, vile and outcast women, thieves, and murderers, civilizes the man eating savage. The responses mark it as a divine book.

(3) It has gained recognition for such principles as:

a. The worth of the individual.

b. The law of mutual love.

c. The sacredness of human life.

d. The duty of internal holiness.

e. The sanctity of the home.

f. Monogamy.

g. Religious equality of the sexes.

(4) It has inspired self-denying labors for human welfare and created hopes in times of sorrow and death.

13. Its own claims.

(1) It claims to be the word of God.

A. In the Old Testament, Ex. **4:12, 15; Deut. 4:2; Jer. 1:7, 9; Eze. 3:4; 33:7**--Such terms as "God said," "The Lord spoke," etc.; occurring 3808 times -- these claims with their fulfillment mark it as divine.

B. In the New Testament.

(a) New Testament writers claimed that the Old Testament was from God, **Acts 1:16; 3:18; 28-25; Heb. 1:1-2; 1 Pet. 1:20-21.**

(b) Paul claimed to speak the word of God, **I Cor. 2:13; 14:37; 1 Thess. 2:13; 2 Tim. 3:16.**

(2) It is then the word of God as it claims to be and a good book, or a false and therefore bad book. But by its fruit it has proven a good book and not a book of lies. We must then accept it as the word of God according to its claim or repudiate it as the worst of all books.

14. Its use and commendation by Jesus.

(1) Christ's attitude toward the Bible decides Christian attitude. If He endorsed it, we must accept it, or reject Him.

(2) Jesus spent most of His public ministry teaching and interpreting the scriptures.

(3) He endorsed many special and miraculous matters in the Old Testament.

a. The three great divisions as writing of Him. Luke. 24:44.

b. The miracle of the manna in the desert, John. 6: 32-35.

c. The story of the destruction of Sodom and Gomorrah, Matt. 10:15.

d. The story of Lot's wife, Lu. 17:32.

e. The historicity of the flood, Matt. 24: 37-39.

f. The historicity of the story about Jonah and the whale, Matt. 12:40; Lu. 11:29-39.

g. The story of the brazen serpent, John. 3:14.

(4) He is either deceived about it, or would deceive us, or it is the word of God as He teaches. We must either accept the Bible He endorsed, or reject. Him for endorsing what we consider false.

15. Two quotations.

1) "The Bible contains the mind of God, the state of man, the doom of the impenitent, and the eternal happiness of believers in Christ. Its doctrines are Holy, its precepts binding, its histories true, and its decisions immutable. Read it to be wise, believe it to be safe, practice it to be holy. It contains light to direct you, food to support you. It is the Christians' character. Christ is its subject, our good is its design, and God's glory is its end."

Finis J. Dake

2) It is "supernatural in origin, inexpressible in value, infinite in scope; divine in authorship, though human in penmanship; regenerative in power, infallible in authority; personal in application; inspired in totality."

Dr. R. G. Lee

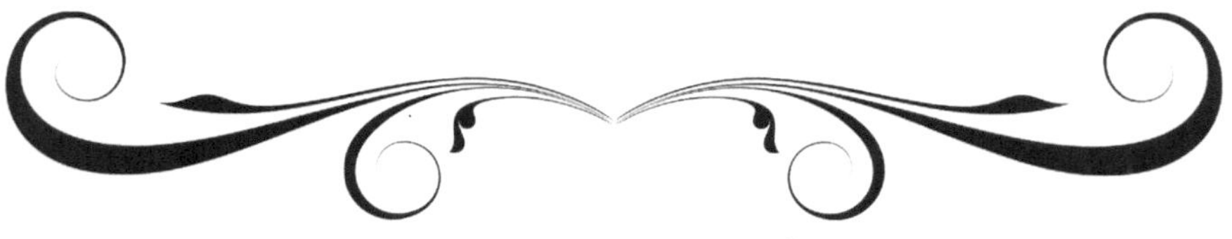

96. Turn To The Bible

When you are in sorrow - read John 14.

When men fail you - Psalm 27.

When you have sinned - Psalm 51.

When you worry - Matthew 6:10-34.

When you are in danger - Psalm 91.

Before Church service - Psalm 84.

When you have the blues - Psalm 34.

When God seems far away - Psalm 139.

When you are discouraged - Isaiah 40.

If you desire to be fruitful - John 15.

When doubts come upon you - John 7:17.

When you forget your blessings - Psalm 103.

For Jesus' idea of a Christian - Matthew 5.

For James's idea of religion - James 1:24-27.

For stirring of Faith - Hebrews 11.

When you feel down and out - Romans 8:31-39.

When you lack courage for your task - Joshua 1.

When the world seems bigger than God - Psalm 90.

When you want Christian assurance - Romans 9:1-30, I John.

When you leave home for labor or travel - Psalm 121.

When you grow bitter or critical - I Corinthians 13.

For Paul's idea of Christianity -II Corinthians 5:15-19.

For Paul's rules on how to get along with men - Romans 12.

When seeking salvation - read Romans 10:9-13.

REFERENCES

This section lists the sources from which the various works were found / where they were first seen, and who the work is attributed to in the original, where known. Where no information is available (works are anonymous) N/A is shown in this list.

1. Miriam, 1871. John Greenleaf Whittier. http://www.poemhunter.com/best-poems/john-greenleaf-whittier/miriam-2/

2. No original work, nor any exact quote http://www.studylight.org/commentaries/phc/view.cgi?bk=42&ch=5&vs=0

3. The Precious Bible / My Old Bible. Author unknown. Multiple sources

4. The Anvil of God's Word, John Clifford. No information on original source. Monument of an anvil and the poem at Orono church. http://archive.bangordailynews.com/2002/07/04/anvil-of-god-finds-home-at-site-of-orono-church/

5. No title. (For man's unceasing quest for God), by Alice M Pullen, 1942. http://www.hymnary.org/hymn/H4F1942/7

6. O' Word of God Incarnate. By *William Waisham How. 1867.* http://www.hymnary.org/text/o_word_of_god_incarnate From the 1867 addition to Psalms and Hymns, edited by How and Thomas B Morrell.

7. N/A

8. Lamp of Our Feet, Whereby we Trace. By Bernard Barton, 1826. Published in 1982 http://www.hymnary.org/hymn/EH1982/627

9. A Bit of the Book. By Margaret E. Sangster.

10. *"Prayer by Richard Crashaw" Poetry.net.* STANDS4 LLC, 2015. Web. 8 Apr. 2015. http://www.poetry.net/poem/30061.

11. The Problem. By Ralph Waldo Emerson

12. Book: Just folks, poem: My books and I. 1917 By Edgar Albert Guest http://www.gutenberg.org/files/941/941-h/941-h.htm

13. N/A

14. N/A

15. Taken from: The Logos, Vol. 44, page 41 http://www.antipas.org/commentaries/articles/my_bible_poem.html

16. Thy Word I Have Hid In My Heart. By Ernest O. Sellers. 1908. http://www.hymnary.org/text/thy_word_is_a_lamp_to_my_feet_a_light_to

17. The Book, by Winfred Ernest Garrison. Page 10 http://www.ctsfw.net/media/pdfs/EberhardPastorBooks.pdf. "Quoted in The Wonderful World of Books, ed. Alfred Stefferud. The New American Library (New York, 1959)"

18. *Youth's Monitor in Verse*, & c, 1803. Holy Bible, Book Divine. By John Burton, Sr. http://www.hymnary.org/text/holy_bible_book_divine#media

19. A Selection of Hymns, by John Rippon. 1787 Exceeding Great and Precious Promises. By "K". Attributed to Robert Keen and George Keith

20. Wonderful Words of Life. By Phillip P Bliss, 1874.

21. Standing on the Promise. By R. Kelso Carter, 1886.

22. Break Thou the Bread of Life. By Mary Ann Lathbury, 1877 (1-2) and Alexander Groves, 1913 (3-4)

23. I Know the Bible Is True. By Baylus Benjamin Mckinney.

24. My Mother's Bible. By Milan Bertrand Williams, 1893.

25. Thy Word is Like a Garden, Lord. By Edwin Hodder. http://library.timelesstruths.org/music/Thy_Word_Is_Like_a_Garden_Lord/

26. Tree of Knowledge, Bible Tree, Facts About the Bible. Various sources, no information. Seems to just be a list of information about the bible with no citations.

27. N/A

28. N/A

29. Gideon's International.

30. Queen Elizabeth II

31. Helen Keller. (n.d.). BrainyQuote.com. Retrieved April 16, 2015, from BrainyQuote.com Web site: http://www.brainyquote.com/quotes/quotes/h/helenkelle152190.html

32. N/A

33. Multiple sources. Most likely by Puritan John Bunyan

34. Sir William Herschel

35. Theodore Roosevelt

36. Most attributed to George Washington but has the authenticity has been disputed.

37. Multiple sources. Most commonly John Sullivan Dwight.

38. Thomas B. Macaulay.

39. Napoleon Bonaparte

40. Abraham Lincoln

41. Refers to a painting by Thomas Jones Barker called "Secret of England's Greatness" in which Queen Victoria is handing a bible to an African king with this statement.

42. Thomas Jefferson

43. William Gladstone

44. Abraham Lincoln

45. Andrew Jackson

46. W.J. Bryan

47. Woodrow Wilson

48. John Milton

49. Human Nature in the Bible. By William Lyon Phelps, 1922.

50. The Rand-McNally Bible Atlas, A Manual of Biblical Geography and History. By Jesse Lyman Hurlbut.

51. N/A

52. Theodore Roosevelt's address on "the bible" in 1901.

53. John Quincy Adams

54. Religion and Philosophy in Germany A Fragment, pg 14-15. By Heinrich Heine. 1882. Heine, Heinrich. (2013). *Religion and Philosophy in Germany: A Fragment*. London: Forgotten Books. (Original work published 1882)

55. By W.E Gladstone.

56. Life and Sayings of Sam P. Jones: A Minister of the Gospel. Chapter 35, page 18. http://www.baptistbiblebelievers.com/LinkClick.aspx?fileticket=N9ZCZUZWwUI%3d&tabid=355&mid=1152

57. Spoken in 1843 by Daniel Webster. Completion of the Bunker Hill Memorial in Massachusetts.

58. Thomas Carlyle

59. Dictionary of Burning Words of Brilliant Writers, page 35. Quote by Charles A. Dana

60. Patrick Henry

61. Ulysses S Grant

62. John Ruskin

63. Thomas Huxley

64. William Henry Seward

65. Lord Tennyson

66. Horace Greeley

67. Robert E. Lee

68. Sir Isaac Newton

69. Johann Wolfgang von Goethe

70. Immanuel Kant

71. Charles Dickens

72. Limited information. Found in a book: "Critical and Miscellaneous Essays, Volume 2, chapter: Novalis, pg 245

73. Jan Christian Smuts

74. Newell Dwight Hillis

75. John Quincy Adams

76. Richard Cecil

77. Fulton Oursier

78. A. Galloway

79. James Waddel Alexander

80. N/A

81. A. T. Pierson

82. Calvin Coolridge

83. N/A

84. Victor Hugo

85. Dwight L. Moody

86. N/A

87. Pope Gregory I / Gregory the Great

88. John Flavel

89. Henry Van Dyke

90. W. A. Criswell

91. Dr. R. G. Lee. The second half is unmatched.

92. N/A

93. Billy Sunday

94. Multiple sources, including J. Newton Brown, but most commonly unsourced.

95 – 15 Two Quotations
By Finis J. Dake
Dr. R. G. Lee.

95. N/A

ABOUT THE AUTHOR

MFON . Effiong Tochukwu obtained his Bachelors Degree {B.SC} Hons, in Pure and Applied Chemistry, from the University of Uyo, in Akwaibom state, Nigeria.

He is married with Kids, and is a prolific writer, mostly of inspirational books and also story books. Currently he is the owner of Insout Services - a life changing book reading and discussion group.

OTHER BOOKS FROM DREAMSTONE PUBLISHING

Dreamstone publishes books in a wide variety of categories – here are some of our other books:-

Coping With Grief

By Penny Clements

Business Strategy :
12 Steps to Business Sanity
How to Optimize Your Profits and Your Time, Grow Your Business and Get Your Life Back Too!

By Kim Lambert

The Father Balance
How YOU, as a Father, can successfully build a career and, at the same time, still keep your marriage and family together !

By Leith Adams

All Books Available on Amazon and other good Bookstores.

DREAMSTONE
PUBLISHING

www.ingramcontent.com/pod-product-compliance
Lightning Source LLC
LaVergne TN
LVHW052255100826
845147LV00001B/53

* 9 7 8 1 9 2 5 1 6 5 4 8 7 *